We arrived at our hotel in Lea-on-Sea early on Saturday morning. The Hotel Vista. Susan and I always stay there. It is very quiet, very friendly and the food is good. I opened the door, and we walked in.

'Good morning, Mrs Brown,' I said.

'Mr and Mrs Reed,' she said. 'It's good to see you again.'

'It's good to be here again,' I said.

'Cup of coffee?' she said. 'Before you go up to your room.'

'Thank you,' I said.

'Where's little Mary?' asked Susan. Mary was Mrs Brown's daughter.

'She's in the garden,' said Mrs Brown and laughed. 'But she's not little! Mary's a tall young woman now.'

'How old is she?' Susan asked.

'Fifteen,' said Mrs Brown.

'Fifteen!' I said. 'Time goes quickly!'

'I know,' said Mrs Brown. 'Now, coffee! Before I forget again.' She walked to the kitchen.

Susan looked at me. 'I love it here, Peter,' she said.

'I know,' I said.

'When did we first meet?' she asked. 'Eleven years ago? Twelve?'

'Wrong,' I said. 'It'll be thirteen years on Tuesday,' I said. 'In the café.'

'Ah, yes,' said Susan, and shut her eyes.

The door opened, and Mary Brown looked in. She was tall.

'Hello,' she said to Susan. 'And hello again,' she said to me.

'Again?' I said.

'Yes. Don't you remember? Yesterday. You said "hello" in the bank.'

'Oh, y . . . yes!' I said, and pretended to remember. 'That was you!'

Mary smiled. 'I'll see you later,' she said. 'Goodbye!'

'Goodbye,' we said. She shut the door. Susan turned to me.

'Why did you pretend?' she asked me.

'I don't know,' I said.

The sun was hot in the afternoon. After lunch, Susan and I walked down to the sea. We swam. The water was cold.

After that, we walked across to Connor's Coffee House. It was a small, quiet café near the sea. *The* café! The place Susan and I first met. We went back there every year.

I opened the door and looked in. John Connor smiled.

'Hello again!' he said to me.

6

7

It was our fourth night at the Hotel Vista. We were at a table in the restaurant, but I did not want to eat. I was afraid. Very afraid. Things were not right in Lea-on-Sea.

On Sunday, it was the old man in the newspaper shop.

On Monday, the man in the bank ...

... and the woman in the cinema.

Yesterday, the girl in the shoe shop.

And this afternoon, the woman in the Italian restaurant. All of them smiled at me and said, 'Hello *again*!'

'A man is pretending to be me,' I said. 'Why?'

'I don't know,' said Susan. 'But it's not important. We're . . .'

'Not important?' I shouted. 'I think it is. I . . . I'm going to the police!'

'No,' said Susan. 'They'll laugh at you. We'll find the man. Lea-on-Sea isn't very big. It'll be easy.'

I looked down. I didn't want to meet the man!

Susan looked into my eyes. She took my hand. 'I'm afraid, too,' she said.

Later that evening, we walked down to the sea. The sun was red and yellow. The water was light blue.

'Today is an important day,' said Susan.

'Important?' I said.

'Thirteen years,' she said. 'You and me! Did you forget?'

'I? . . . Yes, I forgot,' I said quietly.

'Do you love me?' Susan asked.

'Oh, yes,' I said, and turned to her.

'Good,' she said. 'I love you too.'

We kissed. And for the first time on our holiday, I was happy!

Suddenly, Susan moved back.

'Look!' she said. 'It's him! At the café!'

She was right. There was a man with a big nose and black hair. He shut the café door and turned right. At the cinema, he turned right again, and walked quickly away.

'Run!' said Susan. 'We don't want to lose him.'

We arrived at the cinema and looked down the road.

'Where is he?' I said.

'There!' said Susan.

I saw him turn left at the bank.

'Quickly!' I shouted.

We ran across the road after the man.

'Don't go!' I shouted.

But he didn't hear me. We ran to the bank. There, we stopped. I looked up and down the road.

The man was not there.

'Where is he?' I said.

'I don't know,' said Susan. 'But we'll see him again. I know we will. Come on,' she said. 'We'll have a drink at the hotel.'

We walked back to the Hotel Vista slowly. Susan looked in the cafés and restaurants but she didn't see the man again. Luckily!

'Perhaps we'll never see him again,' I said.

'Perhaps,' said Susan quietly.

We arrived at the door of the hotel at ten o'clock. We heard the television. We walked in. We saw Mrs Brown, but she didn't see us.

I smiled. 'Sleeping,' I said.

14

I walked over to the bed. On it, face down, was a photograph. Who was the picture of? I was afraid to look. I took the photograph in my hand and slowly turned it over.

'What the . . .?' I shouted.

'What is it?' said Susan. 'Can I see?'

'You can,' I said. 'But it isn't good!'

I gave her the photo. Susan looked at it, and jumped back. 'But it's you and me!' she said.

'I know,' I said, and looked again.

It was Susan and me. Down at the sea.

'That man!' said Susan excitedly. 'He was there. It's *his* photo!'

Suddenly, we heard a noise. The door opened. And there he was, the man with my face. And he had a gun in his hand.

'Very clever!' he said quietly. 'It was me.'

He shut the door.

'Don't move,' he said. 'Or I'll shoot.'

I looked at the man in horror. I wasn't afraid of his gun – I was afraid of his face! He had my nose, my mouth, my ears, my hair . . .

'You know him!' I said.

'Yes,' Susan answered. 'His name is Stephen Griggs. I worked with him fifteen years ago.'

'I loved you,' said the man. 'We were happy.'

You were, I wasn't! I never loved you!

'You're a bad woman, Susan Barker,' he said. 'You pretended to love me.'

'I did not! And my name is Reed now.'

'Stay back!' he shouted.

Susan stopped.

'Those cold brown eyes,' she said. 'Ugh!'

'Did he always have my face?' I asked.

'No,' said Susan. 'I don't know the game he's playing.'

'You will,' said the man. 'You will.'

He looked at the photograph in my hand.

'That's for you,' he said. 'You can look at it, and remember.'

'Remember what?' I said.

He smiled. 'Your last walk with Susan,' he said. 'Before you go to prison.'

'Prison?' I said. 'Why?'

'Because you shot Susan,' he said.

'I didn't . . .'

'You will,' he said. 'Watch!' And he turned and put the gun to Susan's head.

'NOOOOOO!' I shouted, and jumped at him.

The man shot. I shut my eyes. When I looked again, Susan was on the floor. Dead.

Then, suddenly, the man turned and hit me on the head. It all went black – and I fell down, down, down.

After some time, I opened my eyes again. I remembered.
You shot her!' I said.

'No,' the man smiled – with my smile! 'You shot her.
My plan is going very well.'

I tried to get up, but it was difficult.

'I loved her,' I said quietly.

'I, too,' he said. 'But she was with you. All those
years. Now . . .' He smiled again and looked at the gun.

'Do you plan to shoot me, too?' I said.

'Oh, no,' he said. 'I said, you're going to prison. Perhaps there, you'll understand. For me, Susan was dead before I shot her. Now she's dead for you, too.'

He came over to me, and put his hand over my mouth. Then I heard Mrs Brown at the door.

'What are doing in there?' she shouted.

'Mff . . . mmwff!' I said.

'I shot Susan!' the man answered for me. 'And now she's dead. Dead! DEAD! Oh, Susan, I'm sorry!'

Open the door!

I watched the door. It opened and four policemen walked in. They looked at the dead woman. They looked at the gun in my hand.

The first policeman walked over to me. 'You come with us,' he said.

'I didn't . . . It isn't . . . I can't . . .' I said. I didn't want to go to prison.

'Come with us,' he said again. 'You can talk later. We've got all night.'

'There,' he said. 'Now she'll phone the police. And they'll come – for you!'

He walked over to the window and looked out.

'Remember,' I said. 'You've got my face, too.'

'Not for long,' he said. In horror, I watched him slowly take the mask from his face.

'Now there's only one Peter Reed again. You!'

'But . . .'

'Oh, and one more thing. Here you are . . .'

Before I knew it, the gun was in my hand!

'You can give it to the police,' he laughed.

ACTIVITIES

Before you read

1 Look at the book but don't open it. What can you say about the three people? Look at their eyes. Is this going to be a happy story? What do you think?

2 Look at these words:

afraid   ago   forget   gun   in horror   kiss   last   laugh   mask   pretend   prison   restaurant   shoot   shout   turn   year

Do you understand them? Find them in a dictionary, then write sentences with the words.

After you read

3 Who are they? Give the right names.
   a Susan is . . . . .'s wife.
   b The woman at the hotel is . . . . . .
   c The man working at the café is . . . . . .

4 a Why do Susan and Peter like the Hotel Vista?
   b When did they first meet?
   c Who does Susan see near the café?

5 a Who is in the photograph?
   b Why are the man's eyes important?
   c How does Susan know Stephen Griggs?
   d Stephen doesn't shoot Peter. Why?

6 a What is Peter going to say to the police?
   b What are the police going to say to Peter?

   Talk about these questions with your friends.